Shipwrecks and Sunken Treasures
Coloring Book

by

PETER F. COPELAND

DOVER PUBLICATIONS, INC., *New York*

Introduction

The history of shipwrecks is as ancient as the history of shipbuilding itself. Over thousands of years man has left the wreckage of ships scattered over the ocean floors and the beds of rivers and lakes throughout the world. This wreckage comprises a priceless—because until recently inaccessible—field of study for a new breed of historian, the underwater archaeologist.

A shipwreck is a time capsule, each one unique unto itself, containing all sorts of objects that people used in another age. Each shipwreck has something to tell us about how people worked and lived and built in long-ago days.

Only in the last 150 years was the deep-sea diving suit developed that made the detailed investigation of shipwrecks possible, and then in the post-World War II era scuba-diving gear made man nearly as free as the fishes underwater, at moderate depths, at least.

The development and subsequent popularity of scuba gear has caused concern that wreck sites of historic importance are now vulnerable to destruction by impatient treasure hunters and careless amateurs. Wreck sites have been destroyed—a price, perhaps, that must be paid, for the lure of sunken treasure is strong, almost obsessive. Treasure does exist beneath the sea. There were, in fact, Spanish treasure fleets, heavy with gold and silver, that were sunk in warfare or destroyed by hurricanes, and their remains lie stretched across the seafloor from the coast of South America to Bermuda and, indeed, beyond. Some of these wrecks have been salvaged, and we see pictures of piles of gold chain, stacks of gold and silver coins and bars, and jewels taken from the mud and sea grass of the ocean floor. And there are other treasure ships too numerous to be listed here lost in the oceans of the world.

I was for some years a diver and assistant to the curator of the Department of Underwater History at the Smithsonian Institution, and was associated with various diving expeditions with both treasure hunters and underwater archaeologists. Among my duties was making illustrations of shipwreck structure underwater, drawn with a graphite pencil upon sheets of matte-surface vinyl plastic about the size of small drawing pads. Some of the illustrations seen in this book are done from drawings made underwater at that time.

PETER F. COPELAND

For the Smith family,
Ayanna, Betty, Timothy and Tom

Shipwrecks and Sunken Treasures Coloring Book is a new work, first published by Dover Publications, Inc., in 1992.

DOVER *Pictorial Archive* SERIES

This book belongs to the Dover Pictorial Archive Series. You may use the designs and illustrations for graphics and crafts applications, free and without special permission, provided that you include no more than four in the same publication or project. (For permission for additional use, please write to Dover Publications, Inc., 31 East 2nd Street, Mineola, N.Y. 11501.)

However, republication or reproduction of any illustration by any other graphic service whether it be in a book or in any other design resource is strictly prohibited.

International Standard Book Number: 0-486-27286-9

Manufactured in the United States of America
Dover Publications, Inc., 31 East 2nd Street, Mineola, N.Y. 11501

A diver surfacing. Treasure! A diver has surfaced and is excitedly showing that, at last, treasure has been found on the wreck site: a gold chain, silver coins, the stuff every treasure diver dreams about. At lower left is an enlarged drawing of a doubloon struck at the Seville mint in 1718.

An ancient Egyptian merchant ship. This Egyptian merchant vessel of 2900 B.C. could be moved by sails or paddles. Ships of this type traveled up and down the Nile and even ventured out into the Mediterranean. The wrecks of such ships are now being discovered: they are the oldest shipwrecks in the world. They provide us with valuable information on the lifestyles of Bronze Age people. The vase in the upper left corner is decorated with an oar-powered boat and is believed to be 6,000 years old.

A merchant ship of 1050 B.C. in a North African port. In 1983 underwater archaeologists began studying the wreck of a ship like this one found off the coast of Turkey. The bronze sword at upper right is like one found on the Bronze Age wreck.

Divers gathering amphorae on the site of an ancient Greek shipwreck. Amphorae were the all-purpose containers of the ancient world. Like barrels in a later age, amphorae carried oils, water, wines, all manner of cargoes.

They are seen on shipwreck sites that span many centuries. Here scuba divers are resurrecting a number of amphorae from a tangle of sea grass covering the remains of an ancient shipwreck.

4

A Roman merchant ship in a storm. This ship of A.D. 200 is almost helpless in the grip of a mighty gale and will soon be driven upon the rocks. Her broken bones may be discovered by modern scuba divers and her cargo recovered after 17 centuries on the seabed. The sternpost of this vessel is carved in the Roman fashion in the shape of a swan's head and neck.

The remains of a 9th-century Viking ship. This is a drawing of the Oseberg ship discovered in 1903 buried on a farm in Norway. The remarkable state of preservation of this vessel is due to its having been buried on land as part of the funeral regalia of a Viking chief. A wreck of this age found in the sea would not be in such fine condition. The Viking sword was found buried in a riverbed in England. The inset shows a Viking war vessel of the type that terrorized the coastal towns of northwest Europe for over 200 years.

The *Santa María*, flagship of Columbus, wrecked off the coast of Haiti, Christmas Day, 1492. The *Santa María* was run up on a coral reef and while there was completely dismantled by her crew. Her timbers were used by the survivors to build a fort in which they could dwell until they were rescued.

Early wreck salvors at work. The divers employed by early wreck salvors in the Caribbean were Indian and African slaves, expert swimmers who would free dive, holding their breath for the brief period they were able to work underwater. Here a diver holds a chunk of coral for weight as he plunges to the bottom. His partner holds a line that he has attached to a cannon in the lower hold. The inset is of a deep-sea diving suit developed during the last century and still used in deep-water diving operations.

A diver's fantasy. Here is an underwater fantasy along the lines of Jules Verne's *Twenty Thousand Leagues under the Sea*. The diver has discovered a sunken city (perhaps Atlantis) and a chest of treasure guarded by a ferocious octopus that has entangled the diver in its writhing tentacles. This was the sort of fiction popular in the pulp magazines of 50 years ago. No iron-bound chest would survive immersion in seawater for very long. The remains of the mythical lost city of Atlantis would be buried beneath tons of sand and mud. Octopuses feed mainly upon crabs and lobsters and are among the most timid of undersea creatures.

The *Mary Rose* sinking at Portsmouth, England, in 1545.
The warship *Mary Rose* was the pride of the English fleet when she put to sea to fight the French in 1545. Before she had engaged the enemy, however, she keeled over in a sudden gust of wind and sank as the sea rushed into her open gun ports. Over 400 men were lost out of her complement of 700 soldiers and sailors. The ship had been dangerously overloaded and was in an unstable condition. Several salvage attempts over the centuries succeeded in raising some of her cannon.

The *Mary Rose* on the seabed, 1545. In 1965 a search team discovered the wreck of the *Mary Rose* buried under 15 feet of mud. Excavation of the wreck was not begun until 1979. The hull of the *Mary Rose* was lifted from the seabed and brought ashore in a barge suspended on a steel sup- porting structure. She is being restored at Portsmouth where she was built in 1509. At the upper left we see a pewter drinking tankard, one of the numerous everyday utensils from that faraway time recovered from the wreck of the *Mary Rose*.

Ships of the Spanish Armada of 1588. Philip II, King of Spain, assembled his great fleet of 130 Spanish and Portuguese ships to invade England. At least 20 of the Armada ships were wrecked in an attempt to sail home northward around Scotland after battling the English fleet off the French coast. The invasion was a failure and the battered remnant of the Armada returned to Spain. At bottom left we see an astrolabe, a seaman's navigating device, like one found on the wreck of an Armada ship.

A galleass of the Spanish Armada wrecked off the Irish coast. The stormy rock-strewn coast of Ireland was the grave for many of the proud Armada warships. Here we see the *Girona* shattered on the rocks off the coast of Antrim in a violent storm. Of the 1,300 men aboard the *Girona*, only 9 survived. The wreck site has been located and, although the ship herself has long since disappeared, some cannon, an anchor, a few coins and various other artifacts have been found sheltered among the rocks.

A 17th-century Spanish wreck salvage expedition at work in the Caribbean. Copied from an old print, this drawing shows Indian free divers at work on a recently sunken ship, salvaging her cargo, which has spilled out of her ruptured hull onto the seafloor. Heavy loads of salvaged cargo are raised to the surface vessel by a winch manned by four men with cranks. The sunken ship lies at the foot of the coral reef that sank her.

The sinking of the Swedish warship *Vasa*, 1628. This great Swedish man-of-war sank in Stockholm harbor soon after beginning her maiden voyage. The 180-foot-long ship was top-heavy and, in a sudden gust of wind, the sea rushed into her open lower gun ports. The *Vasa*, like the *Mary Rose*, sank immediately, with all sails set, all flags flying.

The *Vasa* being brought ashore in Stockholm, 1961. Several attempts were made to salvage the bronze guns of the *Vasa*. One such operation in 1664 raised over 50 of her guns, each weighing over a ton, an impressive feat for that time. In 1956 work was begun to raise the entire ship, once it was discovered that the wooden hull was intact and in

remarkably good condition. The teredo worm does not live in far northern waters. Salvage vessels lifted the *Vasa* clear of the harbor floor and set her on a concrete pontoon that was towed ashore. A museum specially built to house and preserve the *Vasa* was constructed around the hull.

A Spanish treasure galleon out of Havana, 1665. This vessel is part of the plate fleet that sailed annually from the New World to Spain, their holds loaded with valuable cargo and treasure. Royal commands sometimes made it necessary for the fleet to sail during the hurricane season, and many a treasure-laden galleon was lost along the coast of Florida or the Bahamas. Some ran aground upon uncharted reefs; others were lost in sea battles with buccaneers. The losses to the plate fleet were formidable. Many of the wrecks have been salvaged, others await discovery by modern-day treasure hunters.

An 18th-century ship just after sinking in the Caribbean. The ship lies upright on the seafloor, her main-topmast breaking the surface. Ballast rocks and cargo spill out of her ruptured hull, her sails have been shredded by the gale that drove her onto a submerged reef. Soon her rigging will decay and her masts sag and fall. Her exposed timber will be attacked by the hungry teredo worm. As the wood rots, wave action and water currents will break the remains apart and they will drop to the seabed to be covered by sand, mud and sea grass.

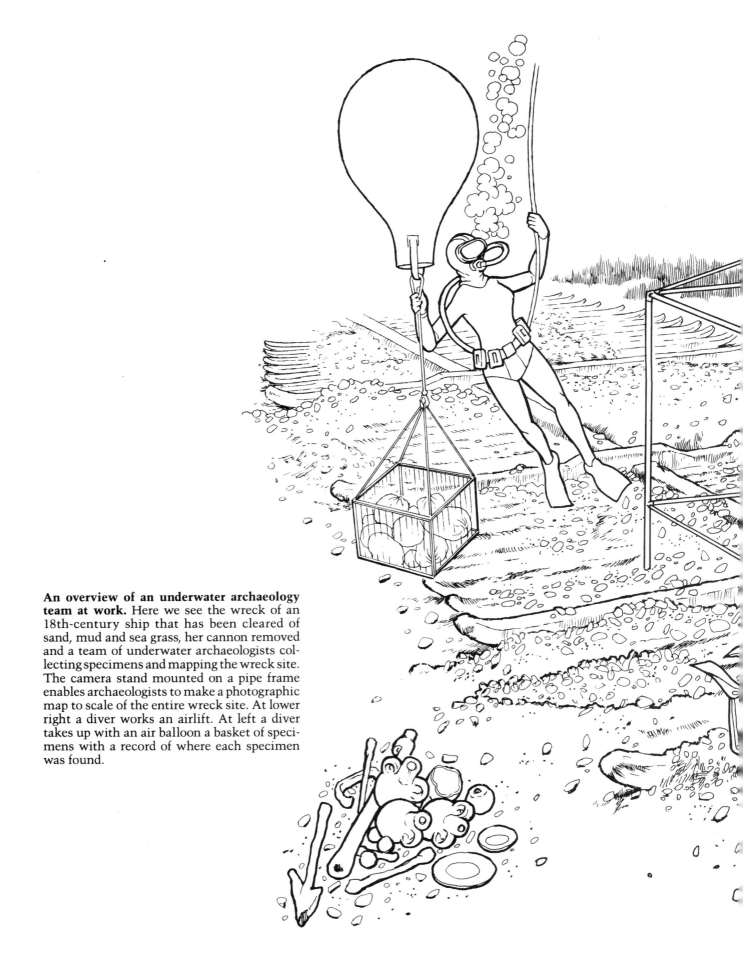

An overview of an underwater archaeology team at work. Here we see the wreck of an 18th-century ship that has been cleared of sand, mud and sea grass, her cannon removed and a team of underwater archaeologists collecting specimens and mapping the wreck site. The camera stand mounted on a pipe frame enables archaeologists to make a photographic map to scale of the entire wreck site. At lower right a diver works an airlift. At left a diver takes up with an air balloon a basket of specimens with a record of where each specimen was found.

A shipwreck after 200 years on the bottom. The only portion of the wooden hull that remains intact is the lower section, which was buried in sand and which the teredo worm could not attack. All that remains visible are the cannon, encrusted in coral, and the ballast stones. Divers will have to remove the cannon and dig down through the sand and ballast to uncover the skeleton of the lower hull before they make any significant finds.

24

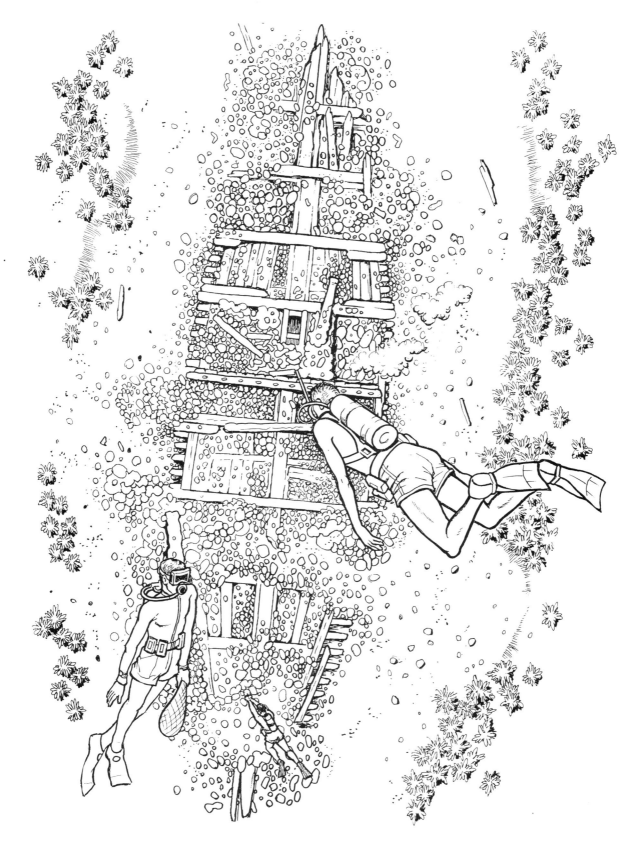

An overview of divers working a cleared wreck site. This is an overhead view of the exposed lower hull of an 18th-century Spanish man-of-war. Most of the ship's cannon have been removed and treasure hunters will now be readying the airlift to work digging holes near the stern section of the hull where bullion was often stored. Others will be examining the timbers for signs that the ship had been burned, which would suggest that the treasure had been removed. Ships that were badly damaged were often burned to recover the iron fittings. The treasure hunters will also be hoping to find items of historical value such as bottles, cutlery, buckles, buttons, etc.

An East Indiaman in a storm. In 1782 the British East Indiaman *Grosvenor* sailed from Ceylon with 150 passengers and crew, and a cargo of jewelry and bullion worth more than two million pounds (about 15 million dollars in today's money). She struck a reef in heavy weather off Cape Province, South Africa, and sank. In 1952 salvors recovered close to a million dollars' worth of gold and silver from the wreck of the *Grosvenor*.

Sharks encountered by divers. 1. Hammerhead shark. Commonly seen in Bahamian waters, it usually grows to between 6 and 12 feet long, although some hammerheads can reach 17 feet in length. It is known to attack people. **2.** Nurse shark. While diving in a dark corner of the Little Bahama Bank, I touched one of these creatures quite by accident. Though the nurse shark is thought to be harmless to man, it was not an experience I would care to repeat. **3.** Great white shark. This white-bellied monster grows to 30 feet long. More attacks on people are reported to have been made by this shark than by any other. **4.** Blue shark. This dark-blue twelve-footer is snow-white on its belly. Found in warm waters in all oceans, there are numerous reports of the blue shark attacking people. **5.** Tiger shark. This shark grows to between 12 and 15 feet long. When young, it has distinguishing striped markings.

Historic diving suits. The art of diving and salvaging ships is an ancient one. One early Greek diver, Scyllias, saved the Greek fleet from disaster at the Battle of Salamis in 480 B.C. when he cut the anchor cables of the ships of the Persian king, Xerxes. An ancestor of the 1665 diving bell (upper right) is mentioned in the writings of Aristotle. The first modern diving suit was designed in England in 1838 (lower left). The Neufeldt and Kuhnke metal diving suit was produced in 1920 (lower right).

Treasure recovered from shipwrecks. Silver cups and cutlery, gold and jeweled crucifixes, gold chains and ornaments from Aztec tombs, a gold coin from the reign of the Byzantine emperor Heraclius are among the treasures recovered from shipwrecks. However, a humble clay cooking pot, a fragment of a shoe, a mark inscribed on the breech of a cannon may have more real historical significance than barrels of coins and jeweled trinkets.

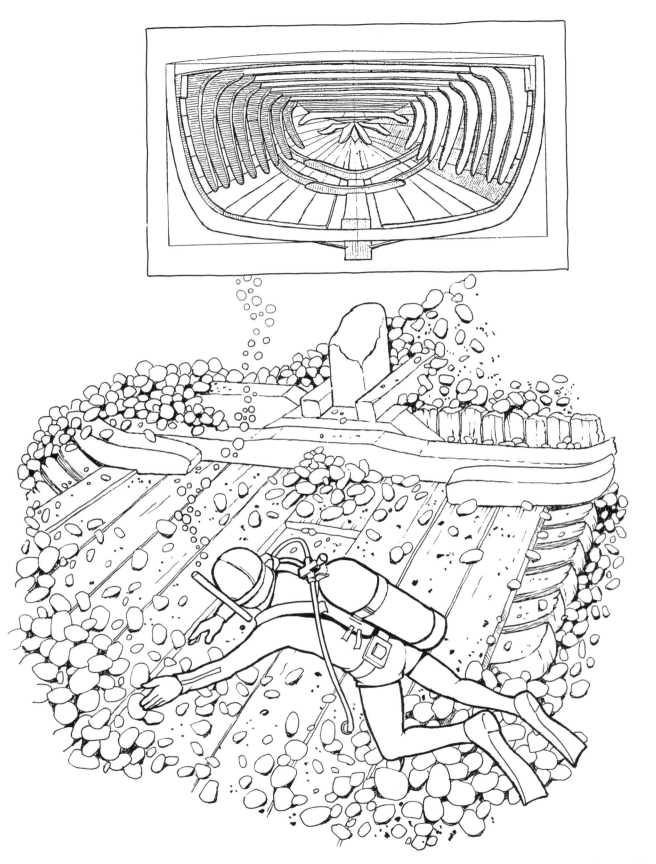

A diver discovers the step and stump of the mainmast of a Spanish wreck. Rough weather delayed work on this Spanish wreck in the Bahamas for a week and after the weather cleared the first diver down discovered that the stump of the ship's mainmast, uncovered by undersea currents, was still seated in the mainmast step. We were eager to remove the stump as legend has it that a silver coin would be inserted inside the mainmast step by the priest blessing the ship when it was being built. In this case, however, no coin was found. At center top can be seen a reconstructed lower hull.

A diver using an airlift. The airlift is an open metal tube into which a jet of air is blown from the bottom. This rush of air causes the airlift to work like a vacuum cleaner: it sucks up sand, mud and small objects. Airlifts come in various sizes. They are essential in wreck clearing, removing tons of sand rather easily and revealing the wreck structure.

Lifting cannon to the surface with air bags. Here we see divers lifting an iron cannon off a wreck site using air bags or balloons. These bags are taken down to the wreck and inflated after the cannon has been rigged for lifting by means of an air hose hooked up to an air compressor on the dive boat.

The sinking of HMS *Pandora*, 1791. The British man-of-war *Pandora* was sent on a mission to the South Pacific to find and bring back the mutineers from HMS *Bounty*. In 1791, *Pandora* took 14 suspected mutineers from Tahiti and, while returning them to England in irons, struck the Great Barrier Reef off northern Australia. The survivors, including 11 of the suspected mutineers, eventually reached the island of Timor in open boats. In 1984 the wreck of the *Pandora* was searched by divers and a number of items including a copper cooking pot, spirit bottles and medicine flasks were recovered. The most interesting find was a silver pocket watch made in 1787, probably the property of the ship's surgeon.

A clipper wrecked in heavy surf off the English coast. The reefs of Annet in the Scilly Isles have claimed many a fine ship. The seabed is strewn with the bones of lost ships—in some places there are layers of wrecks. A recent victim of these treacherous reefs was the 118,000-ton tanker *Torrey Canyon,* sunk in 1967.

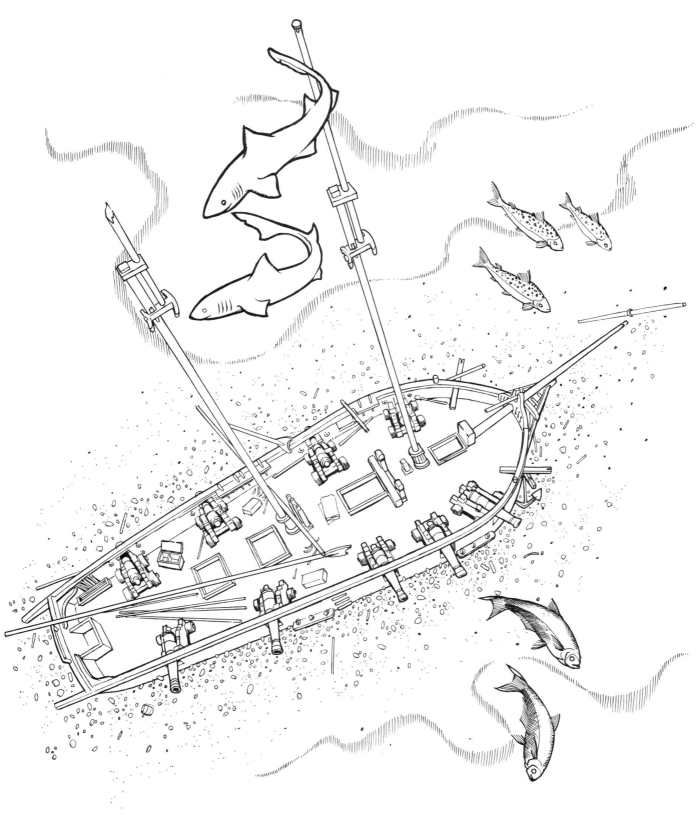

The armed schooner *Scourge*, sunk in 1813 on Lake Ontario. Armed for service with the U.S. Navy in the War of 1812, the schooner *Scourge* sank in a sudden storm while waiting for dawn to fight a British naval squadron on Lake Ontario. The wreck was located in 1973 and a robot craft was sent down to photograph the site. The ship was remarkably well preserved; no teredo worm or ocean currents have disturbed the wreck and it looks much as it did on the day it sank: cannon pointing through gun ports, cannonballs and cutlasses neatly stacked, and the bodies of drowned seamen on the deck. There is hope that the *Scourge* can be raised and preserved.

The sinking of the *Monitor*, 1862. The U.S. Navy ironclad *Monitor*, veteran of a famous fight with the Confederate ironclad *Merrimac*, was heading under tow toward Charleston, South Carolina, to take part in the Union assault on that city during the Civil War, when she sank in a violent storm off Cape Hatteras on 31 December 1862. Archaeologists have located the wreck and photographed it, using a robot craft, where she lies in 220 feet of water. The *Monitor* is lying upside down on the seafloor with her gun turret broken off.

Scuba-diving gear. "Scuba" is an acronym for "self-contained underwater breathing apparatus." Here we see a scuba diver in full wet suit, together with his accessories. The wet suit is made of neoprene, a synthetic rubber. **1.** Scuba tank, about two feet long, weighing about 35 pounds when full. The two-stage regulator gives the diver the exact amount of compressed air needed at the same pressure as the water pressure at any given depth. **2.** Rubber fins or flippers. **3.** Face mask. **4.** Buoyancy compensator or inflatable life vest. **5.** Weight belt. **6.** Snorkel. **7.** Knife.

The sinking of the *Titanic*, 1912. The largest ship afloat, the British White Star liner *Titanic* hit an iceberg on her maiden voyage. She sank with the loss of over 1,500 lives. Ten American millionaires were among those lost.

Seventy-three years later a search team located the wreck and in 1986 a camera-carrying robot craft photographed her where she lies two miles deep in the North Atlantic, 350 miles off the Newfoundland coast.

The Titanic as she looks today. As her stern lifted into the air on that fateful day for her final plunge to the bottom, the *Titanic* broke in two with a terrifying roar. The for-

ward section sank to where we see her here, her bow
wedged into the seafloor. The bow and stern sections rest
on the bottom about 650 yards from each other.

A German U-Boat sinks an English freighter, 1917. German submarines and surface raiders sank Allied ships in all the oceans of the world in the two World Wars. Many of these sunken ships are today visited by curious scuba divers. Twentieth-century steel and iron vessels are cer- tainly more spectacular to dive on than ancient wooden vessels, as they are relatively intact, not buried under the ocean floor. These large vessels form artificial reefs at- tracting thousands of fish and other marine life.

The air-sea battle at Truk lagoon, 1944. "Operation Hailstone" was the name the U.S. Navy gave to the attack on the Japanese fleet at the great naval base at Truk lagoon in the Pacific. The lagoon now holds the wrecks of over 60 Japanese naval and merchant ships sunk by U.S. planes in that World War II attack. The wrecks are those of steel ships of comparatively recent vintage and, although overgrown with coral, they appear intact on the seafloor.

Art McKee confronts wreck pirates. Art McKee, a pioneer scuba diver and treasure hunter, once confronted wreck poachers armed with spear guns who were trying to pillage the wreck of a Spanish galleon that Art had been working off the coast of Florida. Art had a bang stick of his own invention, an underwater gun firing a shotgun shell, which he demonstrated by shattering a piece of wreck timber. The pirates fled, unaware that the bang stick held only one shell.

The dive boat *L. R. Parker*, 1969. Most divers operate on a shoestring budget as far as money and equipment are concerned. The *L. R. Parker* was a tired but fairly typical dive boat in 1969. She was an old converted fishing trawler. Here she is shown on a wreck site off Islamorada in the Florida Keys, her red-and-white diving flag fluttering from the mast atop her bridge, signaling that divers are working down below. Her diving raft is tied up alongside, near the bow. She finally sank in 1971, while working on a wreck site. Those who worked aboard her still remember her fondly.